TRANSITIONS OF WOMANHOOD & CERVICAL CANCER PREVENTIVE CARE THROUGH AYURVEDA

LIVE WOMANHOOD TO THE FULLEST

DR. PRATIKSHA P. RATHOD

I dedicate this book to my beloved parents

Contents

CHAPTER ONE

BACKGROUND

Throughout her life, a Woman undergoes a constant transition from one state to another. Childhood to puberty and menarche brings significant physical, physiological, and psychological changes in a girl. After which, she experiences constant change during the menstrual cycle through phases like proliferative, secretory, and menstrual in her reproductive period of life. The pregnancy and post-pregnancy reversing process bring tremendous metabolic, immunological, endocrinological, and psychiatric changes in a female. Pre-peri and post-menopausal transitions leading her to old age are not devoid of the various phenomena. All these transitions directly or indirectly affect the gynecologic changes and are responsible for cervical health.

Carcinogenesis, or the origin of cervical carcinoma, lies in the transition where the cervical transformation zone changes. As per the studies above, the risk of developing cervical cancer remains at all ages; the highest seems to be in the third decade of life.*

This effort is a novel approach toward the code of conduct and lifestyle during these physiological conditions on cervical care as cancer-protective care.

**Singer A. The uterine cervix from adolescence to menopause. (Br J Obstet Gynaecol. 1975;82(2):81-99. doi:10.1111/j.1471-0528.1975.tb02204.)*

CHAPTER TWO

INTRODUCTION TO THE STATUS OF CERVICAL CANCER IN THE CURRENT SCENARIO

Neoplasia is considered to have an unknown cause. There is no specific nature of management and data of results that can lead to satisfaction. Malignant conditions are emerging as an essential cause of death. Cervix carcinoma is most typical in developing countries and is still the commonest.

Carcinoma cervix (CC) is second on the list of common malignancies. It is the second cause of death in women suffering cancer-related morbid conditions worldwide. Sexually transmitted virus, HPV-Human papillomavirus, is the cause of almost all cervical cancers. The risk factors for cervical cancers are the same as sexually transmitted diseases or infections (STD/STI). Sexually active at the early age of life, multiple sexual partners, first delivery at an early age, multiple pregnancies, smoking, immune-compromised state(e.g., human immunodeficiency virus [H.I.V.] or medicine induced), and prolonged use of O.C. pills. As per modern thought, preventive care should be focused on sex education and awareness of safe sexual behavior. However, in a few areas, contracting HPV is unavoidable for women out of compulsion of social custom. Social customs have become endemic in some regions, encouraging early/child marriages, polygamy, multi/grand parity, and prolonged use of contraception. Poor socioeconomic status, negligible access to medical care, and husbands who have had multiple sexual partners actively or in the past place the women under the high-risk category of cervical cancer. Loose empowerment has an essential role in the significant figure of carcinoma cervix. Health providers also face challenges as these factors are imposed on them. Women's hesitation in seeking health care or education is a big hurdle.

CHAPTER THREE

TRANSITIONS IN WOMEN & EFFECT ON CERVIX

Transitions during womanhood

Physiological and psychological changes.

1. Menstrual cycle
2. Pregnancy
3. Post-partum
4. Premenopause
5. Postmenopause

Effect of transitions on cervical cytology and risk of cervical carcinogenesis

The adolescent period varies in virgin and sexually promiscuous girls. The cervical transformation zone of a virgin is seen under limited physiological changes. The cervical transformation zone, which is atypical, is developed in these girls. In pregnant ladies, particularly in primigravida, the increased size gets squamous metaplastic epithelium in large amounts. It may be the effect of fluid in the vagina with acidic P.H., which is in constant contact with the columnar epithelium of the endocervix.

The effect of the acidic nature of vaginal fluid may contribute to the development of an atypical transformation zone in pregnant. The atypical transformation zone of the cervix has a variable neoplastic potential.

Post-delivery, the atypical epithelium of the atypical cervical epithelium, a neoplastic lesion, may remain as it is or recurs. Minimal changes occur in the physiological transformation zone when childbearing age is over. The last chance may be cervical shrinking at the time of menopause. It suggests the carcinogenesis or origin of cervical carcinoma lies in the transition where the cervical transformation zone changes. As per the studies above, the risk of developing cervical cancer remains at all ages; the highest seems to be in the third decade of life.

CHAPTER FOUR

How the Hormonal Changes During Pregnancy Favor Cervical Carcinogenesis

Low-risk HPV and high-risk HPV are genotypical classifications according to the association with cervical cancer.1 High-risk (HPV) attacks squamous epithelium and causes Ca cervix and other malignancies. Pregnancy can aggravate infection by high-risk HPV (in particular, HPV 16). Pregnancy provides a suitable condition for activation of HPV, persistence, and transformation. Raised estrogen and progesterone levels in pregnancy are responsible for this condition. An imbalanced flora in the vagina calls the infection that favors the development of infectious agents, including HPV. Hypertrophy and congestion in the genital tract is the anatomical modification during pregnancy. It is followed by metaphase. These hormones already influence the cervix's transformation zone (T.Z.). The cervix's local immune micro-environment is altered, sensitizing it to cancer formation. The cervical squamous epithelium is composed of keratinocytes; these are the primary targets of HPV; estrogen and HPV work in synergism which is considered the most potent factor for carcinogenic transformations.

Furthermore, the Mutagenic activity of estrogens can be amplified by viral oncogenes. Progesterone levels which are elevated to maintain the fetus through immunosuppression, are a fundamental process that is the additional risk of acquiring HPV-developed lesions during pregnancy. In pregnancy, elevated progesterone encourages the gene expression of HPV, resulting in more numbers of viral copies.

CHAPTER FIVE

CONDUCT AT VARIOUS STAGES

A Unique school of thought (Ayurveda) and various protocols, code of conduct (mode of living), and diet about cervical care as preventive care is shown in the following table.

It deals with the following factors:-

- Psychological
- Nutritional
- Spiritual

Menstrual conduct and lifestyle*(Rajasvala Charya)*
Pre-conceptional Workup *(Garbhadhan Samskar)*
Antenatal conduct/ Pregnancy care *(Garbhini Paricharya)*
Post-natal Conduct/ Care *(Sutika Paricharya)*

1. Menstrual conduct and lifestyle *(Rajasvala Charya)*

Dos and Donts during menstruation have been narrated thoroughly in ancient texts. Absolute sexual abstinence restricted physical activities, positive thoughts *(Kalyandhyayini),* and avoiding mental exertion are advocated. Regarding food, barley, and milk, rice with ghee, milk, and purified butter *(Ghee)* called *Havishya* is prescribed. Spicy and salty food is restricted.

2. Pre-conceptional Workup *(Garbhadhan Samskar)*

It is advised for both male-female who are planning to conceive. One month of abstinence from sexual activity before intercourse has been recommended. The key intervention is detox procedures, *Panchakarma,* which must be performed on the couple to purify gametes called *beejshuddhi* in Ayurveda. Female consumes black gram in Sesame oil and male take Medicated clarifies butter *(Ghee)* as pre conceptional special diet.

Various spiritual practices are also mentioned as part of the preconception ritual called *Garbhadaan samskar* in Ayurved.

3. Antenatal conduct/ Pregnancy care *(Garbhini Paricharya)*

Absolute sexual abstinence has been recommended by the pregnant lady. Monthwise dietary regime of Milk, Clarified Butter*(Ghee),* Curd,Butter (Navneet) & Anabolic *(Madhur)* herbs with dairy products are recommended. Medicated oil-soaked tampons for vaginal use during the last month have been advised. Medicated oil for rectal administration is prescribed for uncomplicated vaginal delivery. Psychological health care includes avoiding adrenergic activities: E.g.-Aggression, grief & low mood. Indulging into spiritual activities & refraining from scary situations or objects are suggested by the scholars.

4. Post-natal Conduct/ Care *(Sutika Paricharya)*

The typical six weeks duration is the *Sutika* (Postpartum)period. Diet, medicine, and psychological support are vital for post-natal care. Ayurveda post-natal care offers a unique diet protocol, day-wise and region-wise. Vidaridi groups, like anabolic drugs, are included in the dietary medicines. Antimicrobial regimes are used for post-natal care in various forms. During the first 10-12 days, mother and child are kept in well equipped and disinfected room called *Sutikagar* (a Specialized room for mother and baby).

Due importance is given to*Rakshoghna karma* (Disinfection process) for mother and baby.

Local procedures for genital health are mentioned. Sitz bath with Warm *Bala* (sida cardifolia and other herbs) oil-filled chair (*Asandika*) is recommended. Priyangu, like drugs polenta *(Krushara*), is used to foment private parts. Massage of both mother and child is advised with *Bala* oil. Medicated smoke therapy to the external genital area is prescribed. Dietary, medicinal drinks for uterine cleansing, *Panchakol* (5 spices mixture) with warm jaggery water is used for the same. *Lodhra,arjunkadamba,devdaru,beejak Karkandhu* Decoction is used for fast recovery. Avoiding adrenergic activities/stress is advocated.

5. Pre and post-menopause - The last transition phase in women's life.

Long-term post-partum effects hidden before may pop up with the increasing age. Many researchers give Rasayana (Rejuvenation medicine) intervention a thought.

CHAPTER SIX

PROBABLE ROLE OF DIFFERENT CONDUCTS & DRUGS IN PREVENTING C.A. CERVIX -PART 1

As the causative factors suggest,

The Ayurveda mode of living in these transitions mainly focuses on immuno-protection, avoiding coitus, and hence exposure of the cervix to infections. Stress is the main factor that has been taken into consideration, reflecting the emphasis on the psychological health of women during vulnerable phases.

1. Mode of living using menstruation *(Rajaswala charya)*

The main emphasis is on avoiding coitus and keeping oneself aloof from all the things that may lead to any desire for the coitus, even in a psychological state.

Cervix is vulnerable to infections every month during menstruation. Ayurveda scholars have advised abstinence during this period. As per scholars, frequent coitus is prohibited as spermatozoa can act as carcinogenic-nucleic acids to cervical cells. Menstrual health has been received due importance. Menstrual hygiene week is celebrated for awareness purposes.

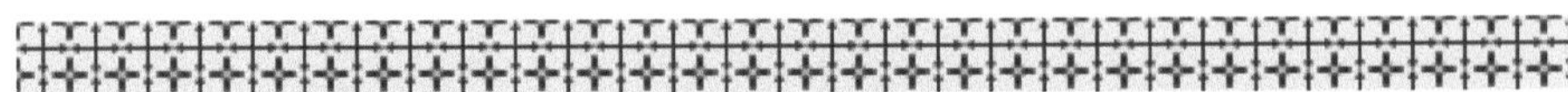

2. Preconceptional Workup *(Garbhadaan Samskaar)*

Panchakarma (Detoxification procedures) and the diet reduce the chances of any genetic abnormalities as the process is indicated for the purification of gametes *(Beejshudhhi)* in both males and females in classics. The compulsion of purifying procedures also leads to healthcare consultation; thereby, marital, premarital, and social stress identification occurs. Screening procedures for cervical cancers like pap smear can be performed simultaneously. Counseling plays a significant role in awareness regarding contraception, sexual behavior, and relationship, a proven solution to stress and S.T.D. to some extent.

During the preconception workup, awareness regardingAyurveda antenatal care *(Garbhini Paricharya)* and necessary medications may help women and their families understand its importance and role in the prevention of various disorders, the bad outcome of pregnancy along with cervical carcinogenesis.

The Ayurveda scholars allow coitus only for reproduction, rejecting the thought of over-sexual activity.

CHAPTER SEVEN

PROBABLE ROLE OF DIFFERENT CONDUCTS & DRUGS IN PREVENTING C.A. CERVIX -PART 2

Pregnancy

As stated before, the risk of cervical carcinogenesis increases during pregnancy. Oxidative stress in the body may exacerbate the condition—potential role of immunological disorders and cervical malignant and premalignant conditions.

Genetic mutations, a hormonal abnormality, poor immune conditions, pregnancy, and post-natal period can trigger the autoimmune system and may lead to high incidence rates of cancers.

Herbs, mediated *Ghee* leading to cervical stability and Immunological changes probably fail to influence cervical changes negatively. In *Sharirasthan* 8, Charak says that if a pregnant woman is *Kalikalahashila* (Quarrelsome), *Shoknitya* (Sad)*, or Amarshini* (Angry), the progeny will be affected in different ways. Avoiding *Manasik Garbhopaghatkar Bhava* (mental stress-related proving situations) may be crucial in preventing pregnancy complications.

Herbal formulations are reported to be rich in antioxidants. Antioxidants can inhibit oxidative damage and prevent inflammatory conditions *(Khanna et al., 2007). Probable role of other conducts & drugs in preventing C.A. cervix.*

Moreover, avoiding neurodegenerative conditions

Herbs used for Antenatal Care

- *Gokshur (Tribulus Terrestris)*

The study in elite rugby league players (2007 May;21 (2):348-53 in Australia) concludes that After five weeks of supplementation of *Gokshura,* strength and fat-free mass increased significantly.

- *Bruhati (Solanum Indicum)*

Bruhati fruits are found to be active against gram-positive and gram-negative bacteria. *(International journal of biological and chemical science).* It acts as a natural antibiotic against the bacteria present in vaginal flora. It has cytotoxic activity.

- *Shatavari (Asparagus Racemosua)*

It has T-cell activating potential in a dose-dependent manner with the best results at 100mg/k bodyweight. *(Gautam M. et al. 2009)*

- *Poonarnava (Boerhavia diffusa)*

It has anti-inflammatory activity *(Bhalla et al.1971).*

- *Vidari (Pueraria tuberosa)*

Antioxidant activityhas been reported *(Pandey N. Journal of Inflammation:2010).*

- *Anantamula (Hemidesmus indicus)*

The free radical scavenging property may be one of the mechanisms by which this is effective in several free radical-mediated disease conditions.

(Conclusion of the study – Evaluation of antioxidant properties of root bark of Hemidesmus indicus R.Br. (Anantamula), B.V.Patel Pharmaceutical Education &Research Development Centre, Thaltej, Ahmedabad, India)

***Ghrita/Ghee* (Clarified butter)**-Anticancerousproperty

Profuse medicated *Ghrita* (oral or rectal) given in A.N.C. acts as a catalyst for absorption of various macro & micronutrients from the placenta; it accelerates Lipophilic action of the placenta and restores fat in the mother. Studies indicate that Ghee in the diet lowers the Prostaglandins levels in serum and decreases the secretion of leukotrienes by macrophages. (*Department of Biochemistry & Nutrition, Central Food Technological Research Institute, Mysore)*

It has a hypocholesterolemic effect. Ghee contains antioxidants, including vitamin E, A, and carotenoids, which may help prevent lipid peroxidation. (*International quarterly journal of research in Ayurveda, Ayurveda 2010 Apr-Jun: 31 (2): 134-140).*

CHAPTER EIGHT

PROBABLE ROLE OF DIFFERENT CONDUCTS & DRUGS IN PREVENTING C.A. CERVIX -PART 3

Post Natal period

The post-pregnancy immune response gets triggered.

(Journal of biological sciences-14:600-604). The post-partum reversal in the code of conduct *(Paricharya)* and medications aim nutrition to women and avoid malnutrition, which may cause *Aama* (toxins) and weaken the digestive system. Specific care is taken till six weeks to 6 months in the post-natal period: oil massage to pacify *Vata*, administration of drugs enhancing the metabolism.

Bath with water lukewarm water boiled with herbs is used. Rice gruels with milk or *Ghee* (clarified butter) are prepared with Anabolic drugs like *Vidari* for 0-7 days after birth. Considering the strength and digestive capacity, rice with meat soup is given after seven days. Seitz bath is given to alleviate pain and local healing.

Kashyap, the great scholar of Ayurveda, has advised following the regional and cultural practices and scientific regimes during post-natal care. Sixty-four post-partum complications *(Sutikaroga)* are mentioned by not following Ayurveda's post-natal care *(Sutika paricharya)*. It includes displacement of genital organs, menorrhagia, neoplastic growths

(Raktagulma), etc. The aim of normal labor is equally essential. If labor turns into difficult labor *(Dushprajata)*, reproductive disorders *(Yonidosh* and *Arugdar)* are long-term complications. Abnormal labor leads to various gynecological disorders.

The drugs used for the post natal care *(Sutika Paricharya)* in Ayurveda possess the following activities.

1. Anticancer activity
2. Bioavailability enhancer
3. Antidepressant antistress action
4. Adaptogenic effect
5. Ulcer healing property
6. Antimicrobial activity
7. Immunomodulatory activity
8. Antitubercular activity
9. Antioxidant property
10. Antidiabetic activity
11. Anti-inflammatory activity

CHAPTER NINE

NEED FOR PREVENTION OF CERVICAL CANCER

Cervical cancer prevention is poorly stated in modern literature. Routine Papanicolaou tests (pap smear)are not practical. An HPV DNA test is not practical currently. It is unrealistic to make the HPV vaccine available to women in developing countries unless funds are provided. However, without outreach programs, these technologies are failed. Outreach programs can educate the population on cervical cancer prevention. It is challenging to prove complex or simple tools practical unless the communities and women do not get the awareness education in developing nations. Education is the only possible measure for prevention. Ayurveda offers a lot more than just sex education. Prevention of cervical cancers through various codes of conduct is the critical solution for the leading cause of death, carcinoma cervix, in developing and developed nations. Social and psychological factors in developing countries make C.A. cervix more prevalent. Customs like polygamy, early marriages, early deliveries, and multiparity can not be ignored.

CHAPTER TEN

MODE OF ACTION OF VARIOUS CONDUCTS & ROLE OF SEXUAL ABSTINENCE

Life-long health of the cervix is a direct result of correct pelvic care. Long term effects of various codes of conduct and drugs play a vital role in women's health.

Changes during the menstrual cycle, viz- proliferation, secretion, and menstrual phases, pregnancy, post-pregnancy six months, menopausal transitions, stressful customs, and associated transitions may bring many risk situations in a woman. Drugs, herbs, lifestyle, dos, and don't contribute to preventing cervical cancers directly or indirectly during the transition phases in the following three possible ways.

1. Preventing infection
2. Bringing controlled cytological changes in the cervix
3. Dealing with stress-induced metabolic, immunological, psychological, and cytological changes.

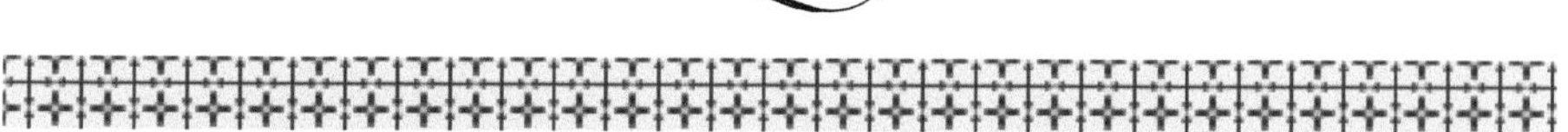

Role of sexual abstinence and male behavior in cervical carcinogenesis

Before marriage, sexual activities (relative risk [R.R.], 1.9; confidence interval, 1.2–3.2) and extramarital sexual activities (R.R., 2.7; confidence interval, 1.5–4.9) of male partners were found risk factors. The risk of carcinoma cervix elevated by 6.9 (CI, 2.3–20.7) in females whose husbands were indulged in sexual relationships both pre-maritally and during the active marriage. Extramarital three or more sexual partners of husbands increased the risk of cervical cancers in wives. (R.R., 3.05; CI, 1.25–12.6). A significant risk factor was a history of sexually transmitted infections pre-marriage (R.R., 2.9) or post-marriage (R.R., 5.9). Sexual abstinence of 40 or more days after a wife's delivery of baby or post-abortion was found protective against cervical cancer. With these results, it can be concluded that male sexual partners play an essential role in the carcinogenesis of the cervix.

(Shaman S Agrawal et al., Role of male behavior in cervical carcinogenesis among women with one-lifetime sexual partner-volume 72, issue 5, 1 September 1993, page 1666-1669)

Bibliography

Scriver CR, Near JL, Saginur R, Clow A. The frequency of genetic disease and congenital malformation among patients in a pediatric hospital. Can Med Assoc Just. 1973 ; 108:1111-5 (PC free article) (PubMed)

Emery AE, Rimoin DL. 2nd ed. New York: Churchill Livingstone; 1990. Principles and Practice of Medical Genetics.

Schneider KA, 2nd ed. Dennisport, Massachusetts: Graphics Illusions; 1994. Counseling about Cancer: Strategies for Genetic Counselors.

Weatherall DJ. 2nd ed. Oxford Oxford University Press; 1985. The new genetics and clinical practice.

Washington DC: N.R. Council, N.A.S., National Academy Press; 1980. Advisory Committee on the Biological Effects of Ionizing Radiation. The effect on Populations of Exposure to Low Level of Ionizing Radiation.

Sharma PV Prof. 9th ed.24. Volume. 3 Chaukhamba orientalia : 2004.Charaka samhita, Sharira sthana :. 424

Sharma PV, Prof. 2nd ed. Chaukhamba orientalia; 2004.Agnivesha.Charaka samhita, Sharira stana ppl. 421-3.3/ 6,7,8,9,10,11,12

Acharya JT. Editor. Sharira sthana 1st ed.32.vol.3 Ayurvediya Granthmala, Chaukhamba Surabharathi Prakashana;1994. Sushrut. Sushrut Samhita of Sushrut with Nibandhasangraha Commentary of Shri Dalhanacharya; p.274.

Acharya JT.Editor. Sharira sthana 1st ed.33. Volume. 3. Ayurvediya Granthmala. Chaukhamba Surabharathi Prakashana; 1994. Sushrut. Sushrut Samhita of Sushrut with Nibandhasangraha Commentary of Shri Dalhanacharya; p.274.

Sharma PV Prof. Editor 9th ed. 6.vol 3. Chaukhamba orientalia; 2004. Agnivesha. Charaka samhita, Sharira stana.;). 412.

Sharma PV Prof. Editor 9thed.32.vol.2 Chaukhamba orientalia; 2004. Agnivesha. Charaka samhita, Sharira stana. P.412

Al-Gazali LI, Dawodu AT, Sabarinathan K,Varghese M.The profile of major congenital abnormalities in the U.A.E. Population. J Med Genet. 1995;32;7-13 (PMC free article) (PubMed)

Shrikant Murthy K.R Prof, translator. Sharira sthan. 2nd edition. 6. Volume. 1. Banglore?,Varanasi: Krishnadas Academy, printer -Chaukhamba press:1994.Vriddhi Vagbhat, Ashtang Hridaya; p.360.8,9.

Sushruta, Sushrut Samhita of Sushrut with Nibandhasangraha Commentary of Shri Dalhanacharya, Sutra sthan 35/9

Acharya JT, editor. Ayurvediya Granthmala Chaukhamba Surabharathi Prakashana; 1st ed. Reprint 1994, Kashyap – Samhita or

Vriddhajivakiya Tantra Sharira sthan 4/1 preached by Maharshi Maricha Kashyap, Summarized then written by his disciple Acharya Vriddhajivaka redacted by latter descendant Vatsya edited by Prof. P.V. Tiwari. Ex. Dean Faculty of Ayurveda., B.H.U. 1st edition reprint 2002,p 112.

Woodman, C. B., S. I. Collins, and L. S. Young. 2007. The natural history of cervical HPV infection: unresolved issues. Nat. Rev. Cancer 7:11-22. [PubMed] [Google Scholar] 2. Singer A. The uterine cervix from adolescence to menopause. *Br J Obstet Gynaecol.* 1975;82(2):81-99. doi:10.1111/j.1471-0528.1975.tb02204.x

Cogliano V, Baan R, Straif K, et al. WHO International Agency for Research on Cancer. Carcinogenicity of human papillomaviruses. Lancet Oncol. 2005;6:2042.

Leemans CR, Braakhuis BJ, Brakenhoff RH. The molecular biology of head and neck cancer. Nat Rev Cancer. 2011;11(1):9–22.

Armbruster-Moraes E, Yoshimoto LM, Leão E, et al. Prevalence of "high risk" human papillomavirus in the lower genital tract of Brazilian gravidas. Int J Gynaecol Obstet. 2000;69(3):223–227.

Correia HS, Cornetta MCM, Gonçalves AKS. Infecção genital pelopapilomavírushumano (HPV) emmulheresgrávidas. Rev Brasil de Genit. 2000;1:14–19.

Romani N, Holzmann S, Tripp CH, et al. Langerhans cells-dendritic cells of the epidermis. APMIS. 2003;111(7–8):725–740.

Beagley KW, Gockel CM.Regulation of innate and adaptive immunity by the female sex hormones oestradiol and progesterone. FEMS Immunol Medi Microbiol. 2003;38(1):13–22.

Karen J Auborn, Craig Woodworth, Joseph A Dipaolo, et al. The interaction between HPV infection and estrogen metabolism in cervical carcinogenesis. Int J Cancer. 1991;49(6):867–869.

Matos A, Castelão C, Pereira da Silva A, et al. Epistatic interaction of CYP1A1 and COMT polymorphisms in cervical cancer. Oxidative Medicine and Cellular Longevity. 2016. 7p.

Chung SH, Wiedmeyer K, Shai A, et al. Requirement for estrogen receptor alpha in a mouse model for human papillomavirus-associated cervical cancer. Cancer Research. 2008;68(23):9928–9934.

Chung SH, Lambert PF. Prevention and treatment of cervical cancer in mice using estrogen receptor antagonists. Proc Natl Acad Sci USA. 2009;106(46):19467–19472.

Chung SH, Shin MK, Korach KS, et al. Requirement for stromal estrogen receptor alpha in cervical neoplasia. Horm Cancer. 2013;4(1):50–59.

Ethel Michel de Villiers. Relationship between steroid hormone contraceptives and HPV cervical intraepithelial neoplasia and cervical carcinoma. Int J Cancer. 2002;103(6):705–708.

Ramachandran B. Functional association of oestrogen receptors with HPV infection in cervical carcinogenesis. Endocrine-Related Cancer. 2017;24(4): R99–R108.

Brake T, Lambert PF. Estrogen contributes to the onset persistence and malignant progression of cervical cancer in a human papillomavirus-transgenic mouse model. PNAS. 2005;102(7):2490—2495.

Marks M, Gravitt PE, Gupta SB, et al. The association of hormonal contraceptive use and HPV prevalence. International Journal of Cancer. 2011;128(12):2962–2970.

Marks MA, Gupta S, Liaw KL, et al. Prevalence and correlates of HPV among women attending family-planning clinics in Thailand. B.M.C. Infect Dis. 2015;15: 159.

Liao SF, Lee WC, Chen HC, et al. Baseline human papillomavirus infection high vaginal parity and their interaction on cervical cancer risks after a followup of more than 10 years. Cancer Causes and Control. 2012;23(5):703–708.

Liehr JG. Is estradiol a genotoxic mutagenic carcinogen? Endocr Rev. 2000;21(1):40–54.

Kanda N, Watanabe S. 17beta-estradiol stimulates the growth of human keratinocytes by inducing cyclin D2 expression. J Invest Dermatol. 2004;123(2):319–328.

Kanda N, Watanabe S. 17beta-estradiol inhibits oxidative stress-induced apoptosis in keratinocytes by promoting Bcl-2 expression. J Invest Dermatol. 2003;121(6):1500–1509.

Nwfield L, Bradlow HL, Sepkovic DW, et al. Estrogen metabolism and the malignant potential of human papillomavirus immortalized keratinocytes. Proc Soc Exp Biol Med. 1998;217(3):322–326.

McMurray RW, Ndebele K, Hardy KJ, et al. 17-beta-estradiol suppresses IL-2 and IL-2 receptors. Cytokine. 2001;14(6):324–333.

Brady H, Doubleday M, Gayo-Fung LM, et al. Differential response of estrogen receptors alpha and beta to SP500263, a novel potent selective estrogen receptor modulator. Mol Pharmacol. 2002;61(3):562–568.

Miller L, Hunt JS. Regulation of TNF-alpha production in activated mouse macrophages by progesterone. J Immunol. 1998;160(10):5098–5104.

Robertson SA, Mayrhofer G, Seamark RF. Ovarian steroid hormones regulate granulocyte-macrophage colony-stimulating factor synthesis by uterine epithelial cells in the mouse. Biol Reprod. 1996;54(1):183–196.

Rando RF, Lindheim S, Hasty L, et al. Increased frequency of detection of human papillomavirus deoxyribonucleic acid in exfoliated cervical cells during pregnancy. Am J Obstet Gynecol. 1989;161(1):50–55.29.

Matlaschewski G, Schneider J, Banks L, et al. Human papillomavirus type 16 D.N.A. cooperates with activated ras oncogene in transforming primary cells. EMBO J. 1987;6(6):1741–1746.

Crook T, Storey A, Almond N, et al. Human papillomavirus type cooperates with activated ras and fos oncogenes in hormone-dependent transformation of primary mouse cells. Proc Natl Acad Sci USA. 1988;85(23):8820–5524.

Moodley M, Moodley J, Chetty R, et al. The role of steroid contraceptive hormones in the pathogenesis of invasive cervical cancer: a review. Int J Gynecol Cancer. 2003;13(2):103–110.

Sima N, Wang W, Kong D, et al. R.N.A. interference against HPV16 E7 oncogene leads to viral E6 and E7 suppression in cervical cancer cells and apoptosis via upregulation of Rb and p53. Apoptosis. 2008;13(2):273–281.

Chung SH, Franceschi S, Lambert PF. Estrogen and ERalpha: culprits in cervical cancer? Trends in Endocrinology and Metabolism. 2010;21(8):504–511.

Chan WK, Klock G, Bernard HU. Progesterone and glucocorticoid response elements occur in the long control regions of several Human papillomaviruses involved in oncogenital neoplasia. J Virol.

1989;63(8):3261–3269.

Chan WK, Klock G, Bernard HU. Progesterone and glucocorticoid response elements occur in the long control regions of several Human

papillomaviruses involved in oncogenital neoplasia. J Virol. 1989;63:4417.

Webster K, Parish J, Pandya M, et al. The human papillomavirus (HPV) 16 E2 protein induces apoptosis in the absence of other HPV proteins and via a p53-dependent pathway. J Biol Chem.

2000;275(1):87–94.

Demerit C, Garcia-Carranca A, Thierry F. Transcription-independent triggering of the extrinsic pathway of apoptosis by human papillomavirus E2 protein. Oncogene. 2003;22(2):168–175.

Webster K, Taylor A, Gaston K. Oestrogen and progesterone increase the levels of apoptosis induced by the human papillomavirus type 16 E2 and E7 proteins. J Gen Virol. 2001;82(pt 1):201–213.

Delvenne P, Herman L, Kholod N, et al. role of hormone cofactors in the human papillomavirus-induced carcinogenesis of the uterine cervix. Mol Cellular Endocrinol. 2007;264(1–2):1–5

Printed by Libri Plureos GmbH in Hamburg, Germany

Ayurveda offers lot more than just sex education. Prevention of cervical cancers through various codes of conduct offered by Indian system of medicine is a novel perspective. Ayurveda is the critical solution for the leading cause of death, carcinoma cervix, in developing and developed nations.

Author bio

M.S. Ayu. Gynaecologist & Obstetrician

Expertise in integrated and traditional medicine.

Counseller and Holistic Antenatal care Coach.

Contact - gynoayurveda@gmail.com

ISBN 979-888772087-6

9 798887 720876

Stuart Broad

England Cricketer

Mr Vivek Kumar Pandey
Shambhunath